A Family

Advent Journey

taken by

_____

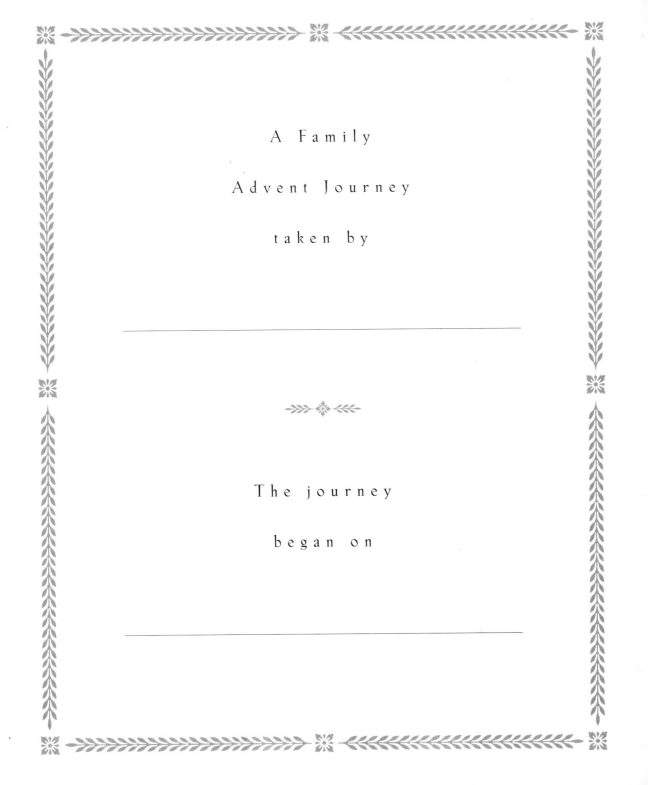

The journey

began on

_____

THE Wonder OF Christmas

A Family Advent Journey

MELODY CARLSON

ILLUSTRATIONS BY DAN BROWN

CROSSWAY BOOKS • WHEATON, ILLINOIS

A DIVISION OF GOOD NEWS PUBLISHERS

The Wonder of Christmas

Copyright © 1999 by Melody Carlson

Published by Crossway Books
A division of Good News Publishers
1300 Crescent Street
Wheaton, Illinois 60187

Illustrations by Dan Brown

Design by Cindy Kiple

First printing, 1999

Printed in the United States of America

LIBRARY OF CONGRESS CATALOGING-IN-PUBLICATION DATA

Carlson, Melody

The wonder of Christmas : a family Advent journey / Melody Carlson.

p.   cm.

Summary: Presents meditations, with discussion questions, for each day up to Christmas and beyond, exploring the meaning of this holiday.

ISBN 1-58134-105-9 (hc : alkaline paper)

1. Advent Prayer-books and devotions--English. 2. Christmas Prayer-books and devotions--English. 3. Children Prayer-books and devotions--English. [1. Advent Prayer books and devotions. 2. Christmas Prayer books and devotions. 3. Prayer books and devotions.] I. Title.

BV40.C55 1999

242'.33--dc21   99-32348

                                                                                                                CIP

In Loving Memory of my grandparents,
Orvil and Elizabeth Haga:

>>> ❖ <<<

As a child of the sixties, being raised by a single. working mom, I had a hunger for family and holiday traditions. Fortunately my grandparents understood these things. And as a result my best Christmas memories revolve around an old-fashioned Victorian house on North Elliott Street and grandparents who went the extra mile to make Christmas wonderful.

I thank you both for all those happy memories—for the hordes of relatives all gathered in one place; for the enormous holly tree centered in the bay window; for those pretty bubbling colored lights; for turkey and sweet-smelling pumpkin pies; for laughter and song; and most of all for love.

I will remember you always, with fondness and love,

Melody
(the youngest grandchild)

Contents

AUTHOR'S FOREWORD

Christmas is by far the most celebrated holiday in our country. By early October, stores everywhere have hauled out their tinsel and trees; and Christmas-related activities begin to fill our calendars almost as soon. With all these expectations and the pressure to perform and conform to the season, how can we preserve the real wonder and awe of Christmas? How can we cut through the clutter and chaos to teach our children the true meaning of this holiday in a significant and memorable way?

My hope is that this book will transport you and your family on a journey that will take you through the ages as together you discover God's purpose in Christmas. And to find God's purpose, we turn to the Bible as our map and guide. By journeying through the Scriptures, starting in Genesis, we begin to see God's amazing plan unfold—a plan for redemption and love and forgiveness—a plan for Christmas!

Designed with thirty-one short, yet thought-provoking readings (one for each day in December), this book offers your family the opportunity to think more deeply about God's enormous plan for mankind. And following each day's narrative you'll find specific questions created to encourage further conversation with your children. In addition, *The*

Wonder of Christmas Activity Book is a fun-filled companion with thirty-one projects and activities meant to enhance and enrich your family's "wonder of Christmas" experience. (I've always found that children remember better with hands-on activities that engage many levels of learning.)

There are various ways you can use this book: at mealtimes, bedtime, or for family devotions. With busy holiday schedules you may choose to read several sections at a time or go through a whole week at once. But however you decide to use this book, I encourage you to keep a family journal (as described in the first section of *The Wonder of Christmas Activity Book*), because I'm sure you'll discover the journal to be a priceless keepsake to treasure and enjoy for many Christmases to come.

My prayer is that this book will not become "one more thing to do during the holidays," but rather a rich blessing for you and your family as together you seek out the true reason for the season—and in turn celebrate the wonder of Christmas!

Blessings!

Melody Carlson

From God with Love

To truly celebrate Christmas, we must journey back in time. We must go back to long, long, long ago. Back to before you were ever born, way back to before Jesus was born, even back to before the time when Adam and Eve first walked in the Garden of Eden. We must go back, back—back to the very beginning of time. We must go back to when God first created the heavens and the earth. And *that* was a long time ago.

But why must we go back into time so far? Because it was then, even before creation, that God began to plan for Christmas.

And way back then Jesus was with His Father, creating the mighty universe, hanging the stars and sun and moon in place, and setting the planets into orbit. It was then that God created this beautiful planet we call home—the earth.

Jesus was there as the rivers and oceans began to flow. As God's Son He made the dark of night and light of day, and then created lush plants and amazing animals to fill the earth with color and life. And Jesus was there when man and woman were created.

And *that's* when God started to plan for Christmas.

Why? you ask. Why did God start planning for Christmas way back then, back at the very beginning of time?

Because God knew.

God knew that we *needed* Christmas. And God knew that Christmas was much, much more than a one-day event. God knew that Christmas would be for all time—yesterday, today, and tomorrow—forever.

So the next time you look at the beautiful things that God created—when you see a majestic tree, a sparkling blue river, a snowcapped mountain, or even a robin flying across the sky—you might think of these things as *Christmas presents* sent to you from God. Because God made them for you to enjoy. He designed them way back at the beginning of time—back when He was planning for Christmas.

You see, God knew we would need Christmas. And He was ready for it.

DISCUSSION QUESTIONS

What do you think of first when you think of Christmas?

What is your most favorite thing about Christmas?

Let There Be Light

One of the first things God created was light. He simply said the words, "Let there be light," and it was done—just like that! That's the way God does things. He says something, and it happens. *Amazing!* But it's important to remember that the reason God created light was because there was darkness.

Most people don't like too much darkness. Sure, it's great for night-time when we're sleeping and our eyes are closed anyway. But can you imagine what it would be like if it was *always* dark? Wouldn't it feel cold and lonely? Dreary and drab? Wouldn't we miss seeing all the beautiful things that God made—the colors of flowers, the faces of our friends? Perhaps one of the best things about darkness is that it makes us really, really thankful for the light.

Did you know that there is absolutely no darkness or night in heaven? That's because *God is light.* There is no darkness in God.

Maybe that's why God sent a special, brilliant star to burn over Bethlehem when Jesus was born on earth. It could be that God wanted to remind everyone that even during the longest, darkest nights, heaven was still full of light. Or maybe God simply wanted to show the people on earth that His Son was coming to bring them the *real light.*

Do you remember how, back at the very beginning of time, God said, "Let there be light"? Could it be that God was actually speaking of His Son? Thousands of years later, Jesus would say, "I am the light of the world" (John 9:5).

Perhaps when God made light, there was a twinkle in His eye as He considered how one day His Son would become *the Light*. And perhaps it was at that moment that God began to plan for Christmas.

Maybe that's why God has given us both darkness and light on earth— so we can understand that our lives are full of darkness without Jesus, but can be full of light with Him. Wouldn't you rather be full of light?

Have you ever noticed how people put up lots of lights at Christmastime? They string lights on houses and stores, on trees and shrubs; why, some people even put lights on dogs! And the twinkling lights look so bright and cheery. They're a happy reminder that God made light for a special reason. Maybe the next time you see those Christmas lights, you'll remember how God said, "Let there be light," and you'll remember that even back then He was thinking of Christmas.

DISCUSSION QUESTIONS

Have you ever been all alone in the dark? Describe how that made you feel.

Name something that light is good for.

Evergreen

Oh, how we love the smell of an evergreen tree. So clean and pure and fresh. It reminds us of a fun walk in the woods—*and* it reminds us of Christmas! The simple evergreen has become an important part of our Christmas celebrations. And there are many wonderful stories and symbolic meanings about Christmas trees that would be fun to learn. But the Bible tells us about a special tree that's even more important than the most beautiful Christmas tree you can imagine.

Let's travel back again to a time long, long ago—back to the Garden of Eden. Do you remember how God made Adam and Eve? He created them in His very own image. He loved them as a father loves his chil-

dren, and He enjoyed talking with them each day. He gave them a beautiful garden to dwell in. And in the center of the garden stood the majestic *Tree of Life*. This amazing tree wasn't any ordinary tree. The Bible
says that those who ate its fruit would have *eternal life*, and this lovely
tree was God's special gift for Adam and Eve to look upon and enjoy
every single day. Can you imagine how beautiful that tree must have
been? More magnificent than the most dazzling Christmas tree ever!

But *this* tree held the gift of eternal life. Do you know what that means?
Eternal life is the promise that death cannot end our lives. Eternal life
allows us to live forever. What an amazing gift that is!

But where can you get eternal life? You can't buy it at the store. You
can't borrow it from your neighbor. Your mom and dad can't wrap it
up and give it to you for Christmas. Only Jesus can give eternal life.
And that is why He is like our *Tree of Life*—for He alone can make
us live forever.

So, what do you think God had in mind when He planted the Tree of
Life in the Garden of Eden? Was He trying to show us what Jesus would
do? Did He want to give us a symbol to remind us of eternity? Perhaps
the Tree of Life was like the original Christmas tree.

Now, when we look at our own Christmas trees, let's remember that

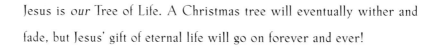

Jesus is *our* Tree of Life. A Christmas tree will eventually wither and fade, but Jesus' gift of eternal life will go on forever and ever!

DISCUSSION QUESTIONS

What does the color green make you think of?

What do you like most about a Christmas tree? Why?

The Big Mistake

Have you ever made a big mistake—done something that you were really sorry for—and then wished and wished that you could do something, anything, to undo it? Maybe that's how Adam and Eve felt after they disobeyed God.

Remember the Tree of Life in the Garden of Eden? Well, there was another tree that was called the Tree of the Knowledge of Good and Evil. It too was a very beautiful tree for Adam and Eve to look upon. With its rich green branches decorated by shiny colorful fruit, it might have been more beautiful than any Christmas tree you've ever seen! But God told Adam and Eve not to eat the fruit of this tree. They could eat from any other tree in the garden except for this one.

Now imagine for a moment that you are standing before a fantastic Christmas tree that is loaded with colorful candies and wonderful toys and pretty presents. But your parents have said, "You may *look* at this beautiful tree, but do not *touch* it or anything on it until Christmas." But you think to yourself, *Christmas is so far, far away, and I want to enjoy those goodies right now!* So when no one is looking, you sneak the candies from the tree and eat them; and you unwrap all the pretty presents, and then you play with all the toys.

Then suddenly your parents walk in and see what you have done.

They see the ruined tree and they know you have disobeyed. And everyone feels very, very bad. You might be so embarrassed that you can't even look your parents in the eye. And you might even feel like they don't love you anymore. Of course they do, but they are disappointed that you disobeyed them.

How do you think Adam and Eve felt after they disobeyed God? We know they were afraid to talk to God. What a sad day that must have been for them. But it was even more sad for God. Before that day He had enjoyed their friendship. They had always walked and talked with Him, sharing their lives with Him. But now they hid themselves in shame.

But God still loved them. And now more than ever God knew that we would *all* need Christmas. He knew that only by sending His own Son could He undo all the bad that had been, and would be, done. Only by sending His Son could He restore the kind of friendship that had been enjoyed in the Garden of Eden. So God continued to plan for Christmas.

DISCUSSION QUESTIONS

How do you feel when you disobey?

How do you think God feels when you say you are sorry?

Just in Time

*O*ne of the most breathtaking sights in all the world is a glorious rainbow! It makes people stop and look and marvel at the sheer wonder of it. But does it ever make you think of Christmas?

Of course, the brilliant colors of the rainbow are pretty enough to decorate a Christmas tree, but there's another reason that a rainbow should remind us of Christmas. Remember back long ago when God told Noah to build that gigantic boat called an ark? It was so huge it would have covered a whole football field! Then God told Noah to load the ark with every kind of animal, both male and female. *That's thousands of animals!* And although it was an enormous task, Noah obeyed God.

Even though it took more than a hundred years to build this gigantic ship, and then to gather tons and tons of food for the voyage, and to finally load all those noisy animals, *Noah never quit*. He never gave up. And then—*at just the right time*—Noah was done! The ark was ready.

And that's when it began to rain. It rained and poured for forty days and forty nights without stopping once! The water rose to make the biggest flood in the history of mankind. The earth became one huge ocean, and anyone or anything not aboard the ark was lost in the flood.

But Noah and his family and all the animals were spared. That huge ark that God had told Noah to build saved them all from drowning in the big flood.

But what does all this have to do with Christmas?

In a similar way, God sent Jesus *at just the right time*. You see, just as Noah knew the flood was coming but had to wait for it, people knew Jesus, the Messiah, was coming to earth and waited hundreds of years for Him. They knew that Jesus would finally rescue them—sort of like how the ark rescued Noah. But only when the time was just right did God send Jesus. And even then, He didn't send Jesus as a powerful king, or even as a gigantic boat, but God sent His Son to earth as a tiny baby, lying sweetly in a manger. But God sent Him *at just the right time*.

And because God sent Jesus at just the right time, all who believe in Him will be saved, just as those who trusted in God on Noah's boat were saved. So the next time you see a rainbow be sure to think of Noah, the ark, *and Christmas!*

DISCUSSION QUESTIONS

Do you think there were times when it was hard for Noah to obey God? Why? Why do you think Noah never gave up?

Making Him Known

For many, many years the story of how Noah and his family were saved from the flood was told and retold. And people rejoiced to remember how God had done this mighty thing. But after hundreds of years, many people began to forget about God, and some even began to worship things that were *not* God.

God loved the people of earth so much that He wanted to be known to them in a special way. And so He decided to create a unique nation that would belong only to Him. The purpose of this nation would be to show the rest of the world what God's love was really like.

To begin His new nation, God chose a faithful man named Abraham. God promised Abraham that his children and grandchildren and all his future relatives would be more numerous than the stars in the sky.

Have you *ever* counted the stars in the sky? *That would make a lot of people!* But the problem was, Abraham was nearly 100 years old when God told him all this, and Abraham had no children! How would he ever have that many descendants? But Abraham's faith was strong—he believed God. That's why some people call Abraham "the father of faith."

Before long, God's promise to Abraham came true—*he had a son!* And in time Abraham had lots of grandchildren, and they had many, many children, and their children had children . . . and on and on it went until God's special nation grew so big that other nations were truly amazed. But *this* was God's plan—that His nation, now called the Israelites, would make God known. And they did.

So, now you're wondering (or maybe you've already guessed),

what does *this* have to do with Christmas? Do you remember that *making God's love known* was the purpose of God's special nation? Now, what was one of the main reasons Jesus came to earth as a baby that first Christmas Day? Do you know? It was *to show God's love to His people!* And that's just what Jesus did! So you see, even when God chose Abraham, He was thinking about Christmas.

DISCUSSION QUESTIONS

How would you feel if someone made you a promise and then broke it? Would you trust that person in the future?

How can you show others what God's love is like?

The Lamb's Gift

Sometimes when we think of little lambs we think of Easter. But what does a lamb have to do with Christmas? Of course, the shepherds came to worship Jesus, and they probably had lambs. But that's not what this story is about. This is the story of a lamb who gives everything to save the people.

Remember God's special nation, the Israelites, the descendants of Abraham? At a time when food was in short supply, they moved to a country called Egypt where food was plentiful. But this place was *not* where God had told Abraham to locate His nation. Even so, the Israelites became very comfortable in Egypt, and they did not return to the homeland that God had given to Abraham.

While the Israelites lived in Egypt, their population increased (just as

God had promised). But the Egyptians grew fearful that they would soon be outnumbered by this unusual nation, and so they made slaves of the Israelites. *Now the Israelites were no longer free!*

How do you think God felt to see His special nation turned into slaves?

For many, many years the Israelites remained slaves. They labored for long hours at difficult tasks, and if they failed to work hard enough they were often beaten. And yet they continued to increase in number. Even when the Egyptian leader, Pharaoh, decided to murder all the Israelite baby boys, they *still* grew in number. Because God had a plan. And because of His plan, a very important baby was spared from death. This special baby was Moses. And God would use Moses to help His people escape the bondage of Egypt.

When Moses stood before Pharaoh, the ruler of Egypt, he demanded that Pharaoh release God's people. But Pharaoh refused. Even after God performed many miracles and punished

Egypt with all sorts of pests and sicknesses, Pharaoh still refused. Finally, Moses stood before Pharaoh and told him that all firstborn Egyptian sons would die if Pharaoh didn't let God's people go. *Again* Pharaoh refused.

God then instructed Moses to have each family in Israel sacrifice a lamb. The blood from these lambs would be used to mark the doorposts of each Israelite home so that when the Angel of Death passed through Egypt, all the Israelites would be spared. Moses and the people trusted God and obeyed what He had told them to do. And because of the lambs' blood, not one firstborn Israelite man or boy died. But many, many Egyptians died. And finally Pharaoh told Moses to take God's people and *go!*

Because of the lambs' blood God spared the Israelites. And yes, even then God was thinking about Christmas, because He knew that one day His Son, *the true Lamb of God*, would also give His blood for the sins of the world! And what a Christmas gift that would be!

DISCUSSION QUESTIONS

What does the word sacrifice *mean to you?*

Why do you think Pharaoh refused to let God's people go?

A Shepherd's Heart

At last the Israelites were free! Pharaoh had finally agreed to let them leave Egypt. But where would they go? What would they do? All they had known their entire lives was slavery. Accustomed to taking orders, they had never learned to think for themselves. In many ways they were like a flock of confused and frightened sheep.

But God had chosen Moses not only to deliver the Israelites from Egypt, but also to *lead* them to where God wanted them to go—*to the Promised Land!* And God had specially prepared Moses for this job. Did you know that Moses had once been a shepherd? He had spent many years tending his father-in-law's sheep out in the wilderness. He probably didn't even realize that this lowly task was actually training him for a very important mission.

In the same way that Moses had once shepherded his sheep, guiding them to food and water and safety, so he now would shepherd Israel from Egypt to the Promised Land. He even used his shepherd's staff to lead the *hundreds of thousands* of people. And like obedient sheep they followed. He used his staff as God divided the waters so they could cross the sea on dry ground. And even as they traveled through the desert, Moses used his staff as God miraculously provided water for all those people.

So, what does Moses' being a shepherd for God's people have to do with Christmas? Well, it's not so unusual to think of shepherds at Christmastime. We often remember how shepherds were the first ones

34

to find the stable and to worship the Son of God. But do you ever wonder why God sent His angels to tell the shepherds *first*?

Could it be that God understands a shepherd's heart? Is it because He loves His people in a way that is very similar to the way a shepherd loves and cares for his sheep?

The Bible is full of shepherds—Abraham, Moses, David . . . and finally Jesus, *the Good Shepherd*. What does God want us to learn from these shepherds? He probably wants us to understand that we are like lost sheep in need of a shepherd.

Remember how the nation of Israel needed someone to lead them into the Promised Land? In the same way, we need Jesus to lead us to heaven. Maybe when those first shepherds knelt before the manger, they understood this. Perhaps on that first Christmas, they knew that baby Jesus would one day grow up to be the Good Shepherd—the One who would lead us all into *God's Promised Land.*

DISCUSSION QUESTIONS

Why do you think God chose Moses to lead His people?

If you'd been an Israelite slave, how would you have felt when you were freed?

A Gift

$\mathcal{L}$ike a faithful shepherd, Moses led the Israelites through the wilderness. But it wasn't an easy task, and the people didn't always want to follow Moses' leadership. After spending their whole lives in slavery, they wanted to celebrate their newfound freedom! But sometimes they forgot it was God who had delivered them. And sometimes they disobeyed God and didn't trust Him.

But God loved the Israelites and had a plan to help them obey Him and to live together peacefully. He called Moses up to the top of a mountain to show him this plan. And when Moses came down, he had a set of ten rules that God had given to him. These rules were God's special gift to the Israelites—a gift that would help them live in a way that would please Him. We call these rules the Ten Commandments, and they are:

Put nothing and no one before God.

Worship God alone, and do not make idols.

Do not use God's name in ways that dishonor Him.

Rest on the Sabbath day, and think about God.

Honor and obey your parents.

Do not murder.

Do not be unfaithful to your husband or wife.

Do not take what belongs to others.

Do not lie to others—or about them.

Do not want what belongs to others.

(Paraphrased from Exodus 20:1–17)

Now, when Jesus came to earth, God's people were still doing their best to keep the Ten Commandments and follow God's law. But Jesus told them there were really just *two* rules to live by. These were:

   "You must love the Lord your God with all your heart, all your soul, and all your mind. . . .

   "Love your neighbor as yourself."

These two rules are also like a gift, because He said if we obey these two rules, we would be obeying the Ten Commandments—and *all* of the other rules. Now, which is easier to remember: ten rules or two? Of course, *two rules* are easier to remember—but that doesn't mean they are any easier to keep. In fact, God knew we couldn't keep them. And that's why Jesus came at *just the right time.*

These two rules are truly a gift, but only if we know Jesus. Because then we have joy and peace—and much, much more! What a great Christmas gift!

DISCUSSION QUESTIONS

What do you think the world would be like if we had no rules or laws?
What rules do you need help keeping?

Redeeming Love

Ruth lived a long, long time ago. You may have heard her story before, but did you know it has something to do with Christmas?

Although Ruth wasn't an Israelite, she married a man who was. But while she was still a young woman without any children, her husband died. She missed him dearly and drew close to his mother, Naomi. But one day Naomi decided to return to her homeland in Israel. Ruth loved Naomi so much she decided to leave her own homeland and family and travel with Naomi to Bethlehem. It was a brave decision for Ruth, for now she would become a stranger in a foreign land.

In Bethlehem, the two women were very, very poor. Each day Ruth gleaned leftovers in the fields of Naomi's relative, Boaz. Only the poorest of the poor did this. They would walk behind the harvesters and pick up any leftover grain. Ruth worked very hard just so she and Naomi could have bread to eat. Boaz admired how this foreign woman labored to care for her old mother-in-law. He told his harvesters to be kind to Ruth and to leave plenty of grain behind for her to pick up each day.

Back then Israel had a custom that if a man should die and leave a young widow behind, his closest male relative should then marry the woman and care for her. This new husband was called a *kinsman-redeemer*. Naomi explained this custom to Ruth, suggesting that since Boaz was Naomi's relative, perhaps he might become Ruth's kinsman-redeemer. Naomi told Ruth to go to the place where Boaz slept during harvesttime and to lie down at his feet. If Boaz covered Ruth with a special cloth, called a mantle, that meant he was willing to become Ruth's kinsman-redeemer.

Boaz placed his mantle over Ruth. He said he was honored to make Ruth his wife! The two were married and soon had a son named Obed. And one day Ruth would become the great-grandmother of the famous King David, and later an ancestor to the Lord Jesus Christ! Quite an honor for a stranger in a foreign land!

Just as Boaz was Ruth's kinsman-redeemer, so Jesus is ours! You see, many of us were not born into the Israelite family (the ones who were already waiting for God's chosen One, the Messiah, to come). But Jesus extended His love and forgiveness beyond the Israelites to the rest of the world, in much the same way that Boaz extended his mantle over Ruth, a stranger.

What a wonderful Christmas gift it is to celebrate that our kinsman-redeemer has covered all of us with His grace and mercy!

DISCUSSION QUESTIONS

What does the word loyal *mean to you?*

Who is your most loyal friend?

Make a Joyful Noise!

At Christmastime we hear all sorts of sounds—church bells ring-
ing, carolers singing, bells jingling, children laughing, donkeys braying in
a live Nativity scene, Christmas music playing in a department store. All
these delightful sounds fill us with a sense of gladness and anticipation of
the special day when we celebrate the birth of our Lord, Jesus Christ!

The Bible says, "How good it is to sing praises to our God." God
enjoys it, and we enjoy it too! Singing praises out loud fills our hearts
with fresh joy. Do you ever feel so happy inside that you just want to
sing but can't think of a song to sing? Why not make up a praise song of
your very own? God delights in our praises—especially the ones that
come straight from our heart.

King David used to make up songs like that for God. They bubbled up out of him just like a fountain. Thank goodness he took the time to write them down! We call those praise songs *psalms,* and many of David's psalms are found in the Bible. Here's a very special one that's full of joy and thankfulness—perfect for Christmastime!

Make a joyful shout to the LORD, all you lands!

Serve the the LORD with gladness;

Come before His presence with singing.

Know that the the LORD, He is God;

It is He who has made us, and not we ourselves;

We are His people and the sheep of His pasture.

Enter into His gates with thanksgiving,

And into His courts with praise.

Be thankful to Him, and bless His name.

For the LORD is good;

His mercy is everlasting,

And His truth endures to all generations.

Psalm 100, NKJV

DISCUSSION QUESTIONS

What is your favorite sound to hear at Christmastime?

Name a special way that you can praise God.

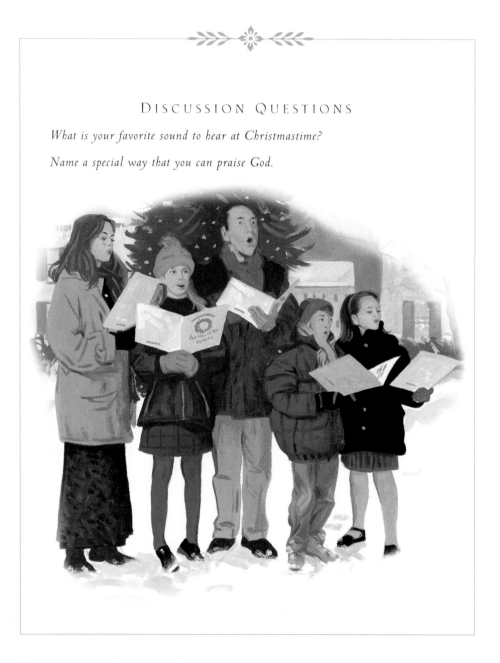

The Promised One

Prophets were people who served and listened to God. Some of the prophets in the Old Testament had strange names like Zechariah, Zephaniah, or Ezekiel. But God spoke through these prophets, showing them important things that would happen in the future—sometimes hundreds, or even thousands, of years before they happened.

And these prophets even predicted Christmas! Through them God let us know that the Messiah (the one we call Jesus) would be a descendant of the great King David and that He would be born in Bethlehem. He also used the prophets to tell us that Jesus would be given precious gifts by the wise men and that a wicked king would try to kill the baby Jesus. But no single prophet knew *everything* about the coming Messiah. Like a giant jigsaw puzzle, each prophet had just a few pieces, and when they were all fitted together they completed the picture.

Prophets knew the Messiah was God's Chosen One—the One who

would save Israel. They described Jesus in many different ways—as a shepherd; a healer of the sick; the living water; one who would set prisoners free; and one who would make the blind to see and the deaf to hear. And when Jesus came, He did *all* these things and much, much more!

The great prophet Isaiah often spoke of Jesus. Isaiah said that Jesus was God's Chosen One and that God delighted in Him and that God's Spirit was in Him. Isaiah also pointed out that Jesus would bring salvation and forgiveness, not only to the Israelites, *but also to the Gentiles!* That meant Jesus would come as the Savior of the *whole* world. This was good news for everyone who wasn't an Israelite. It meant that God had not forgotten them.

That's why we can *all* celebrate Christmas, because God loved the whole world so much that He gave His only Son, so that if you believe in Him you will never die, but instead you'll have everlasting life! What a great Christmas gift!

DISCUSSION QUESTIONS

If you you knew a special secret about tomorrow how would you feel?

If you could tell others the secret would you? Why?

The Long Wait

Remember the prophets who told Israel about the Messiah (Jesus)? Well, it would be hundreds of years before their words came to pass. Can you imagine how hard that must have been for all those Israelites who were waiting and waiting for this wonderful Messiah to finally be born?

How do *you* feel when you have to wait for a big event to come—like your birthday or Christmas? Do you ever count the days until the fun and celebrating will begin? Just imagine that all you know is that *a very important day is coming*, but you don't know for sure *when* it will get here. Imagine that you wait and wait for years and years, you grow up, get married, have children and grandchildren, and *still* that very special day doesn't arrive. That might be how Israel felt as they waited for the

Messiah. Do you think they grew discouraged? Do you think they ever doubted the prophets? Or maybe they even doubted God. It must have been very hard for them to remain faithful.

For over 400 long years, the nation of Israel heard nothing new about the coming Messiah. No prophets spoke of Him. No words were written of Him. Generation after generation passed, and the Messiah still did not come.

The prophet Daniel had predicted that the Messiah would redeem His people after sixty-nine sets of seven years (Daniel 9:24–26). Counting from 444 B.C., which many see as the start of these 483 years, the end of the last year turned out to be the very week that Jesus was crucified! Still, many of the Israelites didn't seem to understand Daniel's prophecy—many of them had little idea of when Jesus would arrive. And as Israel went through all kinds of troubles—slavery, wars, suffering—they longed for the Messiah to come and deliver them. They imagined He would come as a mighty king armed with a powerful sword that would put an end to their enemies. They didn't expect Him to come as a tiny newborn baby, lying in a manger.

And so, as you long for Christmas to come, remember how hard it must have been for the Israelites to wait for *their Christmas* to come. The sad part is that many of them were so caught up in their own lives and human expectations that they didn't even know Christmas had come! That's why we must always keep our eyes on Jesus—we don't want to miss out on Christmas.

DISCUSSION QUESTIONS

How do you feel when someone tells you to "wait"?

What's the hardest thing you've ever waited for?

God Loves Us As We Are

During those long years when the Israelites were waiting for the Messiah, God was preparing the world for Christmas. God knew that Christmas was not only for His chosen people, the nation of Israel, *but for everyone.* The promise of Christmas would wrap itself around the whole world. Christmas was coming for everyone!

God watched as His creation, the people He had made, struggled to understand who they were and God's purpose for their lives. He watched as some nations made up religions that worshiped idols they made with their own hands. Other nations invented all sorts of unusual gods to explain things they didn't understand about life. Some even worshiped animals and trees, bowing down to God's creation without bothering to acknowledge the Creator! *Still, Christmas was coming for everyone!*

God watched as the people He had created lived sinful lives. He watched powerful nations conquer and enslave other nations. He watched people motivated by greed and selfishness hurt others. He watched people who thought they were good lie and cheat and steal and gossip. But all the while God knew that *Christmas was coming for everyone!*

And that whole time God never stopped loving us. Even when those He created turned their back on Him and went their own way, God still loved them. And He was sending His very own Son to prove it. *Christmas was coming for everyone!*

God's love didn't shrink or slow down when mankind turned against Him. And His mercy never stopped. God knew that His forgiveness, compassion, grace, and never-ending love were coming to earth in the

form of one single man—*His Son.* And His Son in turn would pour Himself out for the sins of the world. *Christmas was coming for every-one!* And it was just around the corner!

DISCUSSION QUESTIONS

How does your family treat you when you're being grumpy?

Do you think your family loves *you when you're being grumpy?*

A Great Announcement

*I*magine a glorious angel—tall and powerful, dressed in bright white, and glowing with warmth and golden light—*standing right in front of you!* How would you feel? Shocked? Happy? Excited? Afraid? Would you wonder why the angel had come?

Mary felt concerned when she saw the mighty angel Gabriel standing before her. Of course, she loved and served the Living God, but she was only a young girl and, in the eyes of the people around her, not a very important one at that. *So, why had this magnificent angel come to see her?*

But Gabriel told Mary not to be afraid. He explained that she was *very* special; God had chosen her out of all women to become the mother of the Messiah. And she would name Him *Jesus.*

Mary was astounded! "How can this be?" she asked in wonder.

The angel told her God's Spirit would come upon her, and she would bear His Son. He also explained that her relative Elizabeth, who was very, very old, would also bear a special son. It was almost too much for Mary to imagine.

"But you see," said Gabriel, "nothing is impossible for God."

Mary bowed before the angel. "I am God's humble servant," she said quietly. "Let it be just as you have said."

And in an earth-changing moment, for the first time ever, the almighty,

all-powerful God of the universe Himself took on the tiniest form of man. And God's Son began to grow inside of Mary!

Christmas was truly coming now! And the greatest Christmas gift was miraculously wrapped inside an obedient young woman named Mary.

DISCUSSION QUESTIONS

Describe how you think an angel might look.

What would you say if you saw a real angel?

Another Miracle

*A*fter Gabriel had gone Mary remembered his words about her relative Elizabeth. Was it possible that old Elizabeth was really going to have a baby? "Nothing is impossible with God," the angel had said. So Mary decided to go visit Elizabeth and see for herself.

How do you think Mary felt as she traveled toward the hill country where Elizabeth lived? Just think—all of Israel had been waiting for hundreds of years for God to send the Messiah . . . and now *she* had been chosen to become the mother of God's Son! Was she filled with wonder and awe? Did she want to sing and dance as she journeyed along the dusty road? Did she ponder over this incredible miracle–child that was growing inside her?

Finally her journey was over. She had made it all the way to Elizabeth's house in Judea. When she saw Mary, Elizabeth cried out with happiness, "Blessed are you among women, Mary! And blessed is the child within you!"

Mary was amazed! All was just as Gabriel had said. Elizabeth, though old enough to be a grandmother, was indeed with child. And not just any child. Long ago the prophet Isaiah had foretold Elizabeth's child, saying this was the one who would prepare a way for Jesus (Isaiah 40:3). When Elizabeth saw Mary, the child within her leaped for joy—somehow the unborn baby boy *knew* that Mary was carrying his Lord!

It was a time of miracles, a time of wonder. God was up to something so big, so incredible—something that would change the world forever. Yet God had begun this monumental miracle with something so tiny, so small, so seemingly insignificant. Like a microscopic seed of faith, God chose to use something hidden and unseen to eventually open the eyes of all who would let Him for all eternity. Christmas was coming for everyone!

DISCUSSION QUESTIONS

Have you ever known a special secret that makes you smile just to think about it? What is a miracle? Have you ever experienced one?

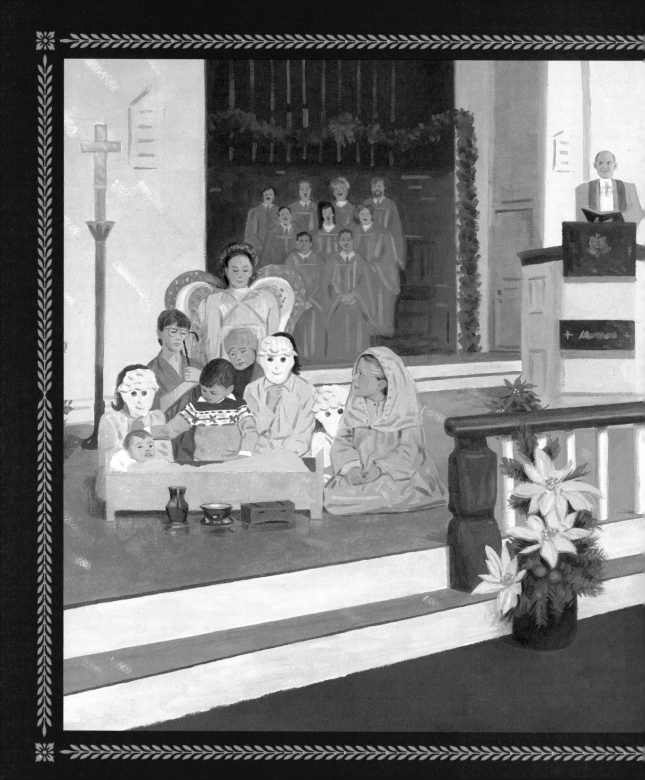

Mary's Joy!

Have you ever been so happy that you felt you might burst like a balloon, spilling your joy and gladness all over everyone around you? Have you ever sung or shouted for joy, or simply jumped up and down in delight?

After seeing Elizabeth, Mary was filled with great joy! She felt like a pot bubbling over with happiness and gratitude. She was so joyful that she couldn't begin to contain it. And so she made up a psalm of praise to God. It went like this:

My heart shouts praises to God!

I rejoice in my Savior, my Lord!

He chose this humble servant girl,

And from now on I will be called "most blessed!"

God, the most Holy One, has done great things for me!

His mercy goes on and on and on—forever!

He is mighty and powerful!

The proud and haughty flee from Him.

Earthly kings fall from their thrones,

but He lifts up the lowly.

He fills the hungry hearts,

but sends the rich away empty-handed.

And now He has helped His servant Israel!

He never forsakes His promise to show mercy.

For He promised our fathers starting with Abraham,

And now His seed will last forever and ever!

Luke 1:46–55 (paraphrased)

DISCUSSION QUESTIONS

What is the happiest moment you can remember?

How do you show your happiness?

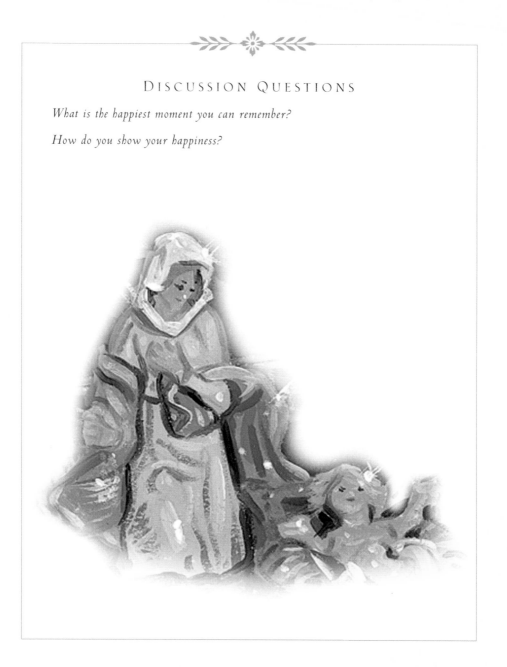

A Dream of Grace

When Mary became pregnant with God's Son, she was engaged to be married to a man named Joseph. So it was only right that he should know about the Messiah. Do you think she was worried about how Joseph would react? Would he be as joyous and excited as she was? Or would this news trouble him? Mary knew that God was in control and that He could take care of this too.

When Joseph found out that Mary was going to have a baby, he was greatly disturbed. He loved the Lord and followed all of His com-mandments. How could Mary expect him to marry her now when it seemed that she did not follow God's law? She was with child. And it was certainly not *his* child. And this story about the angel . . . and the baby being the Messiah—it was just too unbelievable. He couldn't marry someone who did not love God with all her heart, but he also wanted to be kind to Mary.

One night while Joseph was fast asleep, God sent an angel to speak to him. In a vivid dream, the angel explained all that had happened to Mary. He quoted from the prophet Isaiah saying, "A virgin shall bear a child, a son, and His name shall be called Immanuel" (Isaiah 7:14). The angel told Joseph not to be afraid to take Mary as his wife. God

had a plan and wanted His son to have a righteous earthly father to love and to guide Him through boyhood. Joseph had *already* been chosen by God to be that man.

When Joseph woke up, he was completely amazed. He knew without doubt that God had spoken to him. Joseph obeyed God. He took Mary as his wife and lovingly cared for her while together they awaited the birth of God's Son.

DISCUSSION QUESTIONS

What's the best dream you ever had?

Can you think of any ways that you are part of God's special plan?

The Whole World in His Hands

*G*od was still at work, getting everything into perfect order for the birth of His Son—the Messiah. But there were many details and many prophecies yet to be fulfilled. And God had to move men in high places to do exactly what it took to keep this miracle of Christmas in motion. Like putting together a big, beautiful puzzle, God was setting all the pieces into just the right places.

For instance, long, long ago God had shown the prophets that the Messiah would be born in the town of Bethlehem, just south of Jerusalem. Yet Mary and Joseph lived up north in the region of Galilee,

in a small town called Nazareth. It would take them nearly a whole week to travel all the way to Bethlehem. And in Mary's delicate condition, they would *never* have chosen to journey way down there. So how would Jesus—the Messiah—be born in Bethlehem?

God had a plan. The most powerful ruler of the time, Caesar Augustus, gave a decree that every single person in the Roman Empire had to be registered and counted. This was called taking a census. Every man was required to take his family and travel to the place of his family's original home. This meant that, whether he liked it or not, Joseph

had *to* go to Bethlehem. To disobey Roman law was to ask for trouble. And Joseph didn't want trouble.

Imagine how Mary must have felt about going on what would be an exhausting journey, especially with the birth of God's Son so close at hand. Do you think she worried about the health and safety of her son, or did she trust that God knew what He was doing? Maybe she had taken time to become better acquainted with all the old teachings and prophecies about the Chosen One—the Son of God. Maybe she understood and simply smiled when she learned of Caesar's decree, thinking to herself, "Aha! So that's how it will be that Jesus is born in Bethlehem."

Yes, God was working out His plan for Christmas. And He would not allow one single detail to be overlooked. His plan was perfect. His Son was coming soon!

DISCUSSION QUESTIONS

1. Try to count how many living relatives are in your extended family.

2. Where were you born? Where would you like to have been born? Why?

The Long Road

For days Mary and Joseph traveled southward to Bethlehem. There were no cars, no trains, no buses. Most of the time they simply walked, resting briefly here and there along the way. Mary may have ridden a donkey for portions of the trip, but we don't know this for sure. And even if she did, riding a donkey is tiring too. At night they probably camped beneath the protection of trees or stayed in a crowded inn along the way.

Many other people traveled along the miles and miles of Roman roads at that time. All of them were returning to their hometowns to be counted for the census. It was a busy time, and Mary and Joseph weren't the only ones who were on their way home.

Mary was young and healthy, but she was also very large with child. Quite likely, her back ached, and her tired feet were probably sore and swollen. Do you suppose she counted the days until she and Joseph would reach their destination? Have you ever been on a long trip where you kept asking your parents, "Are we there yet?" That must have been how poor Mary felt—*Are we there yet?* And it couldn't have been easy

for Joseph to watch his young bride suffering patiently as they continued on their forced journey to Bethlehem. Surely he did all he could to make her trip easier. Was he worried about her? Or did he trust that God had everything under control?

By the time they reached Bethlehem, Mary must have been totally exhausted. She knew that it was important for them to find a place to stay because in a short time she would give birth. But Bethlehem, normally a quiet town, was also the hometown of all the relatives of King David— *and that was a lot of people!* When Mary and Joseph arrived, the little town was bursting at the seams with thousands of weary travelers *all* seeking a place to eat and sleep.

But God was still at work, putting everything into perfect order for Christmas. He knew exactly when and where His Son would be born. And He would make sure it happened just the way He had planned. Yes, Christmas was coming—and it was coming soon!

DISCUSSION QUESTIONS

If you could go anywhere in the world, where would you go?
What mode of transportation would you use to get there?

The Brightest Star

Many, many miles from Bethlehem, far off in a foreign land to the east, some men noticed a new star in the evening sky. Burning big and bright, this fiery ball of brilliant light was a star of such huge size, such spectacular beauty that these men were amazed!

Now, these were not ordinary men, but wealthy men who spent their time and riches trying to better understand the world around them. Today some call these men magi, some call them kings, and others call them wise men. The Bible teaches that wisdom is worth seeking, and these men were seekers of wisdom. They studied the stars, making maps and charts of constellations, and they even knew the names of stars and could easily spot them in the night sky.

So when this strange, new star appeared in the western sky, they couldn't miss it. And as it reappeared night after night, they became excited and amazed! *What could it be? What did it mean?*

These wise men may have discussed this fantastic star for weeks. Perhaps they sat and marveled over it until finally they could no longer just sit and observe it. They had to go and see what it meant! Never before had they seen such a star—and it seemed likely they never would again. And it is possible that they were familiar with the words recorded in Scripture by Moses: "I see Him, but not now; I behold Him, but not near; a Star shall come out of Jacob; a Scepter shall rise out of Israel" (Numbers 24:17, NKJV). Sure enough, this star did seem to shine in the western sky—maybe over the land of Israel!

Being wise men, they understood this star to be a sign, perhaps even the symbol for a new king—a most important king! As they packed and

prepared for their journey, they wisely included precious gifts fit for the king whose star shone so brightly. Imagine the excitement they must have felt as they began their journey. What would they find? What would they see? All the time, the star continued to blaze brightly before them—like a beacon of hope drawing them to the promise of an everlasting Light.

Do you wonder why God chose to reveal the Star of Bethlehem to foreigners from a far-off land? Was it His way of again showing that Jesus was coming to reach out to the whole world—not only Israel? And did He choose a brilliant star burning in the darkness of night to demonstrate how His Son would soon become the light to a very dark world? Whatever God's purpose, He definitely had it all planned out. And bringing these wise men to Bethlehem was just one small part of His plan for Christmas. And now Christmas was coming fast—it would soon be here!

DISCUSSION QUESTIONS

What's the most amazing sight you've ever seen?

It seems the people in Israel didn't notice the star. Why do you think they missed it?

No Room for the King

*A*s Mary and Joseph slowly worked their way through the streets of Bethlehem, Mary's fragile condition and growing discomfort slowed their journey considerably. It was getting late, and most of the travelers to Bethlehem were already settled in for the night. Only a few latecomers still hurried along the quiet streets, and, like Mary and Joseph, they were eager to find a place to protect them from the coming night.

Joseph went from inn to inn, each time greeted by the same answer—"No room here. Sorry, we're full." His desperation grew with each closed door. *Where would they stay? Where would Mary give birth?*

From draped windows glowed warm, golden lamplight. Brief snatches of laughter and conversation drifted by as road-weary guests were served their evening meal. It seemed that every inn was filled to overflowing with contented travelers, now eating and drinking and catching up on the latest news. A spirit of celebration had taken hold of the little town as family and friends happily reunited after many years of separation.

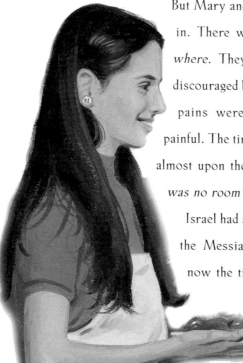

But Mary and Joseph were outsiders looking in. There was no room to be found *anywhere*. They were tired and getting more discouraged by the minute. And Mary's birth pains were growing more frequent and painful. The time for God's Son to be born was almost upon them. *How could it be that there was no room?*

Israel had awaited the birth of God's son—the Messiah—for hundreds of years. But now the time was finally here, and there was no room. No room!

Why? Just think for a moment . . . the most important man ever to be born in the entire universe—and there was no room! Was this a sneak preview of things to come? Would Jesus one day seek a place in our hearts and hear the same answer from us—"Sorry, there's no room"? Let's all pause during this busy, happy Christmas season. Let's all ask ourselves, "Do I have room for Jesus? Have I made room for Him in my life?"

Bethlehem had no room for baby Jesus to be born. All the inns were full. The last door had just been closed on Joseph. What would they do? Where would they stay? Were God's plans for Christmas coming undone? Or did God have an even bigger plan?

DISCUSSION QUESTIONS

Do you think the innkeeper was kind to Mary and Joseph or mean?

If Jesus came to your house, where would you want Him to stay?

Angels on High

All of heaven waited in wonder for Christmas to slowly unfold. Angels watched from on high as God set people and circumstances into perfect place in preparation for the birth of His Son. This was the moment heaven and earth had been waiting for! And it was almost here.

For a moment stop and think about how excited you feel as you help prepare for Christmas, then multiply that excitement by a thousand times, and you might understand how the angels felt that night. They had things to do, places to go, and jobs to perform. All of heaven would do their part to make this the most fantastic, memorable event of all time. God's plan was about to be fulfilled.

So do you think God grew concerned when He saw Mary and Joseph turned away from one inn after the next? Was He surprised and confused about why people didn't welcome the birth of His Son the way the angels would have? Could it be He was a little bit sad that He had sent His Son away from the joys and comfort of heaven to go down to earth and serve man? Of course not! This was *His* plan.

But what about the angels? Were they counting the minutes before they could go to earth and announce the fantastic news? Were heaven's minutes longer than earth's? Did they have to tune their instruments or

warm up their voices? And did they shout for joy when the command was finally given for them to travel to earth?

Did they giggle with nervous anticipation as they made that important flight? Did the brilliant star of Bethlehem light their way? Did they have any problem finding the shepherds out on the hills? Do you suppose they wondered why God first chose to tell the shepherds about Jesus' birth— why had He not chosen a king or a high priest? Or did they, being angels, simply accept these things without question? Oh, the excitement the angels must have felt as they did their part to make Christmas happen!

DISCUSSION QUESTIONS

If you had a very important message to give, how would you share it?

What is your favorite thing to do in preparation for Christmas?

Born in a Stable

Just as Joseph was about to give up his search for lodging, an innkeeper remembered an empty stall in the stable behind his inn. He offered it to the tired couple, and Joseph humbly accepted. By now Mary could travel no further, and her labor pains had grown worse. Joseph knew the stable would have to do.

By lantern light they found their way to the stable. It could be that someone helped them settle in—or maybe they were all alone with only God watching. We don't know these details for sure. Joseph likely spread a fresh bed of straw, laying a thick woolen blanket over the top. The sweet smell of hay may have mingled with the natural scents of animals as cool streams of evening air filtered through the openings in the thin stable walls. In many ways it wasn't a bad place to be. At least it was more peaceful than the noisy, crowded inns.

But why would the Son of the almighty, living God, the King of all kings, be born in a lowly stable? How could it possibly be? And what did it mean? Did Joseph wonder about these things as he tried to make Mary more comfortable? Did he ask himself what God was up to? Did he know that the Son of God had come to serve *all* of mankind? Did he know that Jesus would one day reach out to the poor and the sick, the brokenhearted and down-trodden? Did Joseph understand these things? Did Mary?

Overhead, the brilliant star continued to shine

brightly over the lowly stable. Angels breathlessly waited, listening intently, ready to break into rejoicing. On the nearby hills shepherds rested with their sheep, unaware that their lives were about to change forever.

And then a cry split the night—pure and sweet and clear! And the infant Jesus came into the world, breathing His first ragged breath and experiencing life as a fragile human being. Tiny and vulnerable, weak and dependent. What a strange way for *God* to enter the world!

Mary wrapped the babe in clean white cloths and laid Him in the manger. Did she know that many years later He would be wrapped in a similar cloth and laid in a tomb? Did she understand the greatness of this moment, or did she merely look into her son's dear face and become lost in His bright eyes? Perhaps she cooed softly as she gently held Him close, hiding this moment in her heart to treasure forever.

Christmas had begun. But it was only the beginning . . .

DISCUSSION QUESTIONS

1. Why do you think God wanted His Son to be born in a stable?

2. If you were an animal in the stable where Jesus was born, what animal would you be? Why?

God's Gift to Us

God's Christmas gift to us was *His very own Son.* It was the greatest gift ever!

But how do you measure the worth of a gift? By its price tag? By its size? By how long it took someone to make it? Or find it? Or wrap it? What makes a gift truly valuable?

What if all you had in the entire world was a little, gray kitten? A sweet, fluffy kitten that liked to snuggle in your lap and purr in your ear— a kitten you really loved. But because you loved someone very, very much you decided to give that person your kitten. You tie a bow around the kitty's neck and give your kitten to your friend as a present. You know that you have given the best gift possible. But then a very rich person steps up and gives your friend a pony. The pony looks very important and valuable—you're certain it's a much better gift than your kitten. But what you don't realize is that the rich person has hundreds of ponies, and this was a pony he didn't really like anyway—he just wanted to get rid of it.

So which gift has more value? Just because the pony is bigger, does that mean it is better? Which gift cost the giver more to give? Perhaps we need to rethink the way we measure value, asking ourselves, "How does God measure gifts?"

God gave us the one thing He valued most—His very own Son. That was our best Christmas present ever—*the best He could give.*

Most people celebrate Christmas by giving gifts. Maybe you gave someone a special gift this Christmas— perhaps something you made yourself. Gift giving is a very wonderful part of Christmas because it reminds us all of the greatest gift ever.

But *why* do you give gifts at Christmas? Did you do it just so you will get something back? Maybe you do it because you feel you have to. Could it be you do it so that everyone will think you are a wonderful person?

When God gave us the very first Christmas gift—His Son, Jesus—He did it because He loved us. That's all. He didn't expect anything in return. He didn't do it because He thought He *had* to. He wasn't hoping for lots of compliments. He did it because He loved us and because He knew we needed Jesus.

At Christmas many people talk about us giving something to God. But God really doesn't need anything. We are the ones who need what He gave—His very own Son. If you have never received God's greatest gift—if you have never asked Him to be your Lord and Savior—today would be a perfect day to accept God's very first Christmas gift.

This Christmas take a quiet moment right now to tell Him, "Thank You for giving us Your Son."

DISCUSSION QUESTIONS

What's the best Christmas gift you've ever received?

What's the best Christmas gift you've given to someone else?

Shepherds Watch

Angels erupted with joy—praising, singing, dancing, shouting! *Glory to God—at last, at last, the Son is born!* All of heaven rejoiced. Jesus Christ, the Messiah, had finally come to save the earth! What a celebration—what an unforgettable moment in time!

But down on earth, all was quiet and calm. Life went on as usual. No one yet knew that Christmas had come. On a nearby hillside, shepherds peacefully bedded down with their flock of sheep, bundled up against the night air. Tired from the day, they were ready to go to sleep. Perhaps they watched the incredible star burning brightly in the dark velvet sky. Perhaps they even spoke in hushed tones of *the coming One*, wondering in their hearts if the Messiah might possibly come within their lifetime. Then suddenly, from out of nowhere, a majestic angel burst upon them! Trembling with fear, the shepherds drew back from the angel, almost afraid to look upon his glory and splendor. *Who was this magnificent being? And why was he here?*

With power and authority, the angel spoke to the shepherds. "Do not be afraid!" he said, explaining that he brought good news—*great news!*— not only for the shepherds, but for all mankind. "On this very day," said the angel as he pointed at the city below them, "right down there in Bethlehem, the Savior, Jesus Christ, has just been born. And this is how you will know that it's Him: you will find the babe wrapped in white cloths and lying in a manger."

The shepherds stared in open-mouthed wonder. And in the next moment, the night sky exploded with many, many angels. They were singing and shouting and praising God.

"Glory to God in the highest!" they shouted. "And on earth, let there be peace and goodwill to all mankind!" And as quickly as they had come, the angels were gone.

Did the shepherds wonder *why* the angels had chosen to share this fantastic news with them? Do you think they stood around discussing all that had just happened? Or were they so excited that they simply ran down the hill as fast as their tired legs would carry them, in search of the newborn Savior? The Bible says *they went quickly* to find Him.

And when they found Jesus, just as the angel had described, they fell to their knees to worship Him. They didn't doubt He was the Messiah. They simply rejoiced in Him. And then the shepherds went all over telling everyone about what they had seen. Perhaps that's one reason God told the shepherds *first*. He knew they'd do a good job of spreading the news. And perhaps God also knew that shepherds would feel a special connection to the One who would someday be called *The Good Shepherd*. Or perhaps God wanted to take one of the lowest positions in life, a shepherd, and exalt it to the highest, a worshiper of Jesus. After all, God had always shown a fondness for shepherds—remember Moses and David?

Christmas was here. And now it was entering the hearts of men and women and boys and girls.

DISCUSSION QUESTIONS

Why do you think God sent the angels to tell the shepherds first?

How do you think the shepherds felt when they saw the angels?

Wise Men Seek Him

Remember the wise men from the East who had spotted the star of Bethlehem? Remember how they immediately left their homeland to search for the newborn king? Their camels were loaded with gifts to present to the child, and they traveled for days and days before they even reached the region where Jesus had been born.

Being intelligent men, they stopped in Jerusalem to ask for directions. They went to the palace of King Herod, thinking that since he was a king, Herod might know the whereabouts of this newborn king. But when Herod heard whom the wise men were seeking, he grew troubled. He was extremely jealous and was afraid of what might happen. *What if this new king is going to replace me?* he must have thought.

Just the same, Herod called in his own scholars, those who understood the words of the prophets, and asked them if they knew where this new

king might be born. Of course, they knew—it had been written long, long ago. They explained that a Ruler would rise out of Bethlehem, and He would be a Shepherd to His people.

Herod then told the wise men they would find this king in Bethlehem. And he asked them to come back to his palace after they found where the new king was so he could go and worship Him too. But do you think that the jealous King Herod truly wanted to worship Jesus? Or was this just a trick?

The wise men continued on to Bethlehem where they finally found Joseph and Mary—and with them Jesus! Their hearts overflowed with joy when they saw the small child. And they immediately fell down to

worship Him. Although they were foreigners, they understood that this was truly the Son of God.

They presented the child with costly gifts. They gave Him gold, a symbol of royalty; frankincense, a symbol of worship; and myrrh, a symbol of death. And before they departed, they were warned in a divine dream that King Herod planned to harm the child; so they left for their homeland without returning to Herod's palace.

Soon afterwards, an angel appeared to Joseph, instructing him to take Mary and Jesus to Egypt, where they would remain safe. The generous gift of gold given by the wise men would provide for the small family while they stayed in Egypt.

Shortly after their departure, the wicked King Herod sent soldiers to kill all the baby boys who had been born in Bethlehem. But Jesus was safe. God was taking special care of His Son. You see, Christmas had just barely begun. And God wasn't finished.

DISCUSSION QUESTIONS

Why do you think King Herod was so mean and wicked?

If you were one of the wise men, what gift would you have given to baby Jesus?

Words of Life

esus didn't remain a young boy. He grew up and became a man. And when the time was right, He was baptized by His cousin John (remember Elizabeth's baby?), and His preaching and teaching and healing began.

From then on, Jesus began to teach people about God. He used every opportunity to remind His listeners about God's kingdom, as if not wishing to waste a single moment. Do you think Jesus knew His time on earth was limited? You see, as an adult He had about three years to show the world His Father's love. That wasn't a whole lot of time. Many pastors will spend their entire lives trying to teach others about God. Jesus had a lot to do in a very short while.

First of all, Jesus gathered a special group of men called disciples. He knew if He taught them well, they would continue to teach even after He was gone. He spent most of His time with these close friends. He told them many meaningful stories and explained many things about God that were hard to understand. These men also watched as Jesus taught huge crowds and performed many, many miracles. Like the time He fed thousands with just a few pieces of bread and a few fish. Or the time He walked right on top of the sea. Or the many times He made

blind people see or crippled people walk. Jesus' disciples didn't know that Jesus would only be with them a short while.

As He taught His disciples, Jesus gave two commands. He said to love God with everything within us, and to love our neighbors as ourselves. It sounds simple, but it's not always easy—and Jesus knew we'd need His help to obey His commands.

He also used many different

names to describe Himself. He called Himself the Bread of Life, The Good Shepherd, The Light of the World, The Vine, The Door, and many, many more names. And some of these many names had been used before—remember how the old prophets foretold of the coming Messiah? So, it was vital that Jesus become all these things in order to fulfill those predictions.

But Jesus had another reason for using these names. These names are like word-pictures that we can see in our minds and easily recall. They help us to remember *who* Jesus is and *what* He is like. Think about it—when you hear that *Jesus is the Good Shepherd*, what do you see? Do you imagine a loving shepherd caring for His little lamb? Do you realize that little lamb is *you*? These word-pictures are precious gifts for us—we can turn to different ones in times of different needs.

DISCUSSION QUESTIONS

If you could change your name, what would you change it to? Why?

What is your favorite name for Jesus?

The Greatest Gift

You may think that by now Christmas is over. Maybe in your house the tree has already come down, and the decorations are all neatly packed away. But we're still not finished with our *journey to Christmas*. In fact, the greatest Christmas gift is yet to come. It's not wrapped in pretty paper or tied with a beautiful bow. At first glance some may even think it is ugly. Because death can be ugly.

Jesus said, "The greatest love is shown when people lay down their lives for their friends" (John 15:13). But what does that really mean? Remember when we talked about God's first Christmas present and what a precious gift that was? Well, there's only one gift with a greater value.

And that's the gift that Jesus gave when He willingly laid down His life. It was a gift of the truest and purest love.

Jesus, *the Son of God—the King of all kings,* was tormented and whipped, beaten and mocked by mere earthly men. His gentle hands, which had touched and healed so many, were now pierced through with spikes. And His feet, which had traveled all over the region to spread the message of God's love, were also driven through with spikes. Then Jesus was hung on a cross for all of Jerusalem to look upon. It was the slow and embarrassing death of a lowly criminal. But while on the cross, Jesus forgave His murderers, and then He died. The Son of God was killed by the people He had come to save.

And in that bitter moment the sky grew black, and all of earth shuddered and shook with pain—it was this world's darkest hour.

Do you ever wonder why God allowed this to happen to His own beloved Son? Why didn't God just send down an army of angels from heaven and let them put a stop to it? It's because God already had a plan in the works—

remember, it was *His plan for Christmas*, and it started at the beginning of time. And allowing His Son to die—to be punished for our sins—was the only way the people He created could be saved. Even the prophets knew of this plan. They described the very time and place and exactly how it would happen (Psalm 22; Zechariah 12:10–13).

So, in many ways, it should not have been a surprise. And yet it was a jolting shock to those who already served and loved Jesus. All they knew was that God had allowed their dear leader, their best friend, to die.

But God's plan for Christmas included this sad day—this darkest moment. God had planned from the beginning to surrender His Son's life so that once and for all there would be a way for us to be totally cleansed from our sins and completely forgiven. Jesus' death paid this high, high price so that everyone who believes in Him can live with Him in heaven—forever! What gift could possibly be greater? Or more costly? That was the cost of Christmas. And God was willing to pay it.

DISCUSSION QUESTIONS

What is the hardest thing you've ever done for someone else?

How does it make you feel to hear about how Jesus died?

Final Victory

So, Jesus was dead, His work on earth finished. He had paid the debt for everyone's sins. *Paid it in full.* But God was *not* finished. Not yet. His perfect plan for Christmas was not complete. Because God is God, and in the end He will have the final victory.

Grieving loved ones had laid Jesus' broken body in a rich man's tomb just as the old prophets had foretold (Isaiah 53:9). With barely enough to time to anoint His body with myrrh (remember the gift from the wise men?), they quickly wrapped Him in white linen cloths and left to mourn. Each one sadly went on his or her own way (Zechariah 12:12). Lost and brokenhearted, their hope and joy had perished with their Lord in the same moment that He had died on the cross. Life as they knew it was over.

But on the third day after His gruesome death, something miraculous happened—*Jesus rose from the dead!* All the angels rejoiced in heaven and on earth. Jesus' stunned disciples and loved ones rejoiced too. Their hope and joy returned to them—in a greater way than ever imaginable! It was a time of wonder and celebration—a time of thanksgiving and great gladness.

Jesus met with many of His friends. He took time to eat and visit with them, and to teach them about things yet to come. He even gave them an important command; He told His disciples to go *all over the earth and tell everyone about what God had done* (Matthew 28:18–20).

Then it was time for Jesus to go—time to return to His Father's home

in heaven. But before He left He gave His followers some big promises. He promised that they would have power and authority and that His Spirit would remain with them. And He promised, "I will always be with you—even until the end of time."

And Jesus' promises all came true. His disciples taught God's truth with life-changing power. Thousands and thousands of people believed in Jesus and were baptized. His disciples healed the sick, made the blind to see, and did many, many other amazing miracles.

Even now, although Jesus is back in heaven with the Father, His Spirit remains with all who receive and believe in Him. God lives in the hearts of every person who trusts in Him. What a truly amazing Christmas gift that is! One we can enjoy every single day of the year. It may very well be the best one so far.

But there is still *one more* . . .

DISCUSSION QUESTIONS

Do you want to have Jesus' power in your life?

How do you think you can have His power?

Our Home on High

*B*efore Jesus left the earth, He made a special promise. He said, "I must leave now to prepare a place for you, but after that I'll return for you. Then I'll take you back with Me, and we'll live together—forever" (John 14:2–3, paraphased). *What a fantastic promise!* Just think, right now if you believe in Jesus, He is making you a special home in heaven—and you will be with Him forever and ever!

Our final Christmas gift (as far as we know now) will be our wonderful *home on high*—a place where we'll always be with God. And that's a gift that will keep on giving and giving—throughout all eternity! It's a gift that will be fresh and new each morning—a gift beyond the most wonderful things we can imagine.

In heaven all tears and sadness will be replaced with great joy and peace. The lame will run and leap and maybe even fly! The blind will see beauty unlike anything ever seen on earth, and the deaf will hear the music of angels.

Heaven will be better than having Christmas every day! More fun than living in Disneyworld! More exciting than flying to Mars! We cannot begin to dream how amazingly awesome heaven will be. But we can be

certain that Jesus will keep His promise to come back and take us to heaven with Him. Jesus has never broken a single promise. He fulfilled every single word of prophecy promised by the prophets. He kept every promise He made to His disciples. And He will keep His promise to us too!

And when we arrive in heaven, there will be a huge, gigantic, unbelievably magnificent celebration. It will be like mixing your best birthdays, Thanksgivings, Christmases, and New Year's Eve's parties all together, and then multiplying those by a million. It will be spectacular—the biggest event in history!

Aren't you glad that God began planning for Christmas way, way back—back in the beginning of time? He knew all along just what He was doing. Even in the darkest moments, God had a perfect plan. And when we finally get to heaven, we'll all bow down to worship and praise and thank Him—just because we love Him so much!

Until then, we need to remember that Christmas isn't only about a single day—it's about God's perfect plan to save the world through His beloved Son. And just as God unfolded Christmas from the beginning of time, we too can unfold Christmas every day of our lives. We can always celebrate all that He has done, and we can also look forward to all He has yet to do! So, Merry Christmas—for the rest of your life!

For God so loved the world

He gave His only begotten Son,

That whoever believes in Him

Should not perish but have everlasting life.

John 3:16 (NKJV)

DISCUSSION QUESTIONS

Describe what you think one small part of heaven will look like.

What do you think you will do first when you get to heaven?